DEATH AND DYING: THE UNIVERSAL EXPERIENCES

By

Dana G. Cable

Specialized Studies, Inc.
P.O. Box 854
Frederick, Maryland 21701

ISBN 0-914547-00-3

DEATH AND DYING: THE UNIVERSAL EXPERIENCES

By

DANA G. CABLE

TABLE OF CONTENTS

To Sylvia
With love and
my heart's thanks

Foreword

For nine years I have been teaching courses on death and dying and presenting seminars to professional and lay audiences. During this time, countless books on death and dying have appeared. One may well ask, "Why another?" Clearly, some excellent material has emerged in these other volumes. However, many of them have been oriented toward research and intensive academic study.

I believe there is a need for a book in this field designed for three audiences. First, this book is meant to serve as an overview for those working in the health-care fields. Today's professional training for medical personnel, clergy, and counselors spends relatively little time dealing with death-related issues. It is hoped that this book can fill this void.

Secondly, this book is appropriate for students studying death and dying in academic settings. It provides an orientation which should be useful regardless of the future vocational aspirations of the student.

Third, I have seen a strong desire on the part of the general public for a book which covers, to some degree, all of the death-related issues we face in our daily lives. This book attempts to do so.

Needless to say, no one book can provide all the information relevant to the field. Nevertheless, it can provide a broad perspective of the issues which exist today. In the chapters which follow we will explore the current attitude toward death and dying in the United States. We will examine the way in which our attitudes develop in childhood and how these attitudes change across our life span. We will further look at the care of the dying patient and the role the health-care professionals play in such care. Finally, we will examine the grief process and the rituals which surround death.

The content of this book is derived from a variety of sources. Some comes from my own study in the field. But the majority comes from my experiences teaching, lecturing, and working with both the terminally ill and grieving individuals. These people have really been my teachers.

I cannot close this introduction without thanking those who helped so much in making this book a reality. My wife, Sylvia, spent many long hours over the typewriter working from my sometimes confusing recordings and notes. Without her gentle, and sometimes not so gentle, urgings, this book would never have come to fruition. My friend, Russell Beaton, suffered through the punctuation and spelling many times to correct my errors. To them, my grateful thanks. But in the final word, any errors are mine alone.

The American Approach to Death

American society today views death far differently from any other time in history. Our society has become one often referred to in the literature as a death-denying society (Kastenbaum and Aisenberg, 1976). What is it that promotes this view of death denial?

Historically, death was accepted as a natural part of life. The average life expectency one hundred years ago was only forty-seven years, as compared to the mid seventies of today. Thus, death was a reality from early life.

At the turn of the century, most families experienced the death of a child, since over half of all deaths occurred under the age of fifteen (Bureau of the Census, 1978). This is in sharp contrast to the small number of childhood deaths we experience today.

More importantly, death was a family experience. When individuals died, it was at home in their own beds, surrounded by family. Following a death, the family prepared the body and held the viewing in the home. At the cemetery, family and friends filled in the grave. Throughout the death and the funeral, the entire family participated in what happened. This was a time of death acceptance.

If we examine the world around us today, it is possible to see many instances supporting a death-denial hypothesis. If we look at the literature to which we expose children in early life, we often see death-denial. Individuals in children's stories fall asleep, disappear, but rarely die. In our adult language today, we see few references to death. We use euphemisms which tend to mask the reality of death. We talk about slumber rooms and eternal sleep rather than death; we pass away or expire, but we don't die. We buy caskets with hundred-year guarantees. We often find death segregated in our society today where individuals are placed in special rooms when death is near. Bodies are removed from institutions only when doors are closed or during those hours when other people will not be upset or disturbed. We even see death-denial existing in our approach to jokes about death, such as the widely-told jokes dealing with St. Peter at the Pearly Gates. Somehow this denial makes it a much more unreal experience.

Why have we developed such a denial approach to death? Perhaps in part we believe that if we deny something strongly enough it will disappear. We often tell individuals that, if they hurt themselves and they simply don't think about it, they won't feel the pain. Are we treating death this way, too? If we deny death long enough, do we believe that it will disappear from our lives? Can we avoid death for ourselves? Some of our denial may be related to a sense of personal failure. Death becomes that one great event in life over which we have no control. It will happen to us no matter what we do. We deny death because our drive for life is so strong that life becomes something to hold on to; death becomes that which destroys.

A further reason for death-denial today is our rapid advance in medical technology. Pacemakers, organ transplants, by-pass surgery, life support equipment—all of these imply the ability to forestall death, making it easier to deny its reality.

Perhaps denial is a healthy process. We do not want to create a world of individuals who constantly contemplate their deaths, who think always about the end of life rather than life as they are living it now. However, despite the positive aspects of denial, we clearly want and need to promote a society which recognizes the inevitability of death and deals with it accordingly.

We do find in our society certain elements that suggest death acceptance. Many of us buy life insurance policies, we write wills, we make plans for the time when we will die. We are exposed to death constantly on television. We see cemeteries and funeral homes and funeral processions. We read obituaries in the newspaper. We attend memorial church services. We do have a great deal of exposure to death, but it may be that death has become so over-exposed in its own way that that too becomes a denial for us. It may be that we accept death because that is a normal and adaptive thing to do. Death is around us all the time. Every time we walk out of our houses in the morning, get into our cars, ride in an airplane, or eat a meal, death is always a possibility.

For some people, death is a necessity in that it promotes a sense of fulfillment in their lives. Somehow we learn, even in the early parts of our lives, to value more those things that have an end. When we take a vacation in the summer, part of the reason we appreciate it so much is because we know it will end, and so, we must enjoy it now. Is it not possible that death does the same thing for us? The recognition of life's finite quality consciously or unconsciously somehow makes us more appreciative of the experiences which we have now, of life as we live it now, and gives us that sense of fulfillment.

In the past two decades there has been a renewed interest in death and dying. The works of Herman Feifel (1959) and Elisabeth Kubler-Ross (1969) sparked a resurgence of concern with the needs of the dying and in issues related to death and dying. This, too, has moved us toward a more accepting approach to death.

In the American society of the 1980's, we face mortality constantly in a world fraught with changes: the Bomb, political assassination, national terrorism, and drug abuse. All of these are reminders to us of death: death may strike us at any moment, individually or collectively. Death may even strike those we love.

In the last fifteen years, death has become a very academic and theoretical issue. We find courses on death and dying taught in colleges and universities throughout the country. It is very good to see this kind of movement, but one of the dangers is that we become too academic or too theoretical. We must learn to look at death in a practical sense. It is an experience common to all of us. It is universal, inevitable, and inescapable. All of us will die someday. All of us will face the deaths of loved ones. It is time that we all learned to open the door to death and to look death in the face.

REFERENCES AND/OR ADDITIONAL READINGS

Feifel, H. (Ed.) (1959). *The meaning of death*. New York: McGraw-Hill.

Kasenbaum, R. & Aisenberg, R. (1972). *The psychology of death*. New York: Springer.

Kubler-Ross, E. (1969). *On death and dying*. New York: Macmillan.

U.S. Department of Commerce, Bureau of the Census. (1978). *Social indicators III*. Washington, D.C. Author.

Attitudes Toward Death and Dying

For most people, the most common emotions aroused by death are fears. They begin in childhood, and today those fears continue into adulthood.

To be sure, fear of death is an important adjustment factor. Without the fear of death, we would risk our lives unnecessarily, and premature death would probably be the result. It is, in effect, necessary for human existence, but in many instances our fear of death becomes so strong that we avoid even the mention of the word. We prefer to use words such as "pass on," or "depart this life," or "promoted to glory" to represent death rather than the word "death." If someone close to us should talk of his or her own death—that is an aged grandparent or someone like that—our immediate reaction is to reassure them that this won't happen for a long time; it is not in the near future for them. Perhaps part of the fear comes from the image of dying that used to be reflected in the words "death agony," which gave us a spectacular and distorted picture of what death is all about.

Some people would argue that every fear is a fear of death. If we think about the typical phobias that different people experience—fear of heights, fear of closed places, and such—what is it that they are really fearing? If they are at great height, they may fall. If they are closed in, they may not be able to breathe. In a sense, all of these phobias represent some kind of a basic fear of death. In reality, fears of death seem to be universal. We see them represented in all cultures in one way or another.

It is important to differentiate between what we call "fear of death" and what might be called "fear of dying." When we speak of death, we are talking about a state of being. We are alive now. Someday we will no longer be alive; we will be dead. On the other hand, dying implies a process, a way of getting from that state of life to the state of death.

Different professionals would speak of that process in different terms. For example, a philosopher might well speak of dying as something that begins at the moment of birth. A physician may talk about dying as that which takes but an instant. A psychologist, one working with the terminally ill, may believe that the dying process is best represented as that period of time from the moment one begins to recognize failing health or receives a diagnosis of a life-threatening illness. Most people tend to show a far greater fear of dying than they do of death itself. In an interesting study done in 1936, M. H. Means gave a series of words to college women, asking them to express the degree of fear that each word represented to them. The results showed greater fear of the words "snake" and "cancer" than the word "death." What does this mean to us? Snakes and cancer imply dying as opposed to death. If this is the difference, then, between the two words, what are some of the specific fears that go along with each of these factors?

Looking first at factors in the fear of death, probably one of greatest fears for most people, when they think of death, is the general fear of the unknown. As a young child is afraid to go into a dark room unless someone will go in and turn on the lights, so we see in people a fear of death as the greatest of all mysteries, the greatest unknown. It is impossible for us to imagine our own death or what death may be like. Thus, despite whatever our religious beliefs may be, the fear of the unknown in death persists.

Secondly, we tend to have a fear of death in terms of our apprehension over the loss of things, things that we enjoy in life. As we experience life, we collect objects and items. Over a period of time, those objects, because of the relationships we attach to them, become as important as we ourselves. Thus, the highly treasured vase on the table in the living room may not be just a vase; rather it is an integral part of a person, and that person would be very upset if something happened to the vase, if it were broken or damaged beyond repair. To stop and contemplate one's own death, to recognize that at some point in time all these things will be lost, can, indeed, be a frightening experience. This may well explain why funeral directors frequently receive unusual requests from people to have certain objects buried with them, things that simply cannot be given up or lost forever. This may also be part of why it is that we write wills, because it is important to us to know what will happen to some of those objects when we die. It may also be that, as we talk with dying patients, we can sometimes calm some of their fears of death by providing them with the knowledge that those possessions will be valued by someone else after their death.

A man in his nineties, who had a very large miniature collection, was greatly relieved when his son-in-law finally was able to ask the old man if he would leave the collection to him in his will. The miniatures had been lovingly accumulated over many years. Each bottle had a story attached to its acquisition; each bottle had been carefully catalogued. Clearly, this collection was a source of pride and joy to its owner. That simple request was, in fact, an affirmation of the father-in-law as a prized and valuable human being.

Another factor in our fear of death is the fact that it signifies the end of our opportunities to achieve our goals and to finish projects which we hold dear. Human beings work in a very interesting way. Few of us function totally in the here and now. Rather, despite what we may be doing at the moment, part of our attention is turned toward goals that we have established for ourselves down the line, from something as routine as fixing dinner this evening, to the vacation we plan this summer, to finishing a graduate degree finally. Each time we near one of these goals, we set some new goal for ourselves. When we have to stop and contemplate our death, we find, in effect, that we have a fear of goals going unfinished, that we will no longer be able to set and maintain those goals for ourselves. This can be very frightening. It is very interesting, in working with elderly patients, that we see much less fear of death. One of the things the elderly will frequently tell us is, "I've lived my life. I did the things I wanted to do." Death is not as frightening to them because they have fewer goals left to strive for.

Another aspect of our fears may relate to the sense of isolation and separation that death implies. We have a need to relate to other people. Death is seen as the ultimate separation. In a sense, we fear the aloneness of death. It could be said that death would not be as frightening if we could take everyone else with us.

Punishment is another aspect of our fear of death. Despite our religious orientation, most people, religious or non-religious, may at times question what comes after death. The possibility of an existence that continues, and that part of that existence could be a hell, could be frightening to us. People looking back over their lifetimes might find certain things that they have done which may or may not deserve punishment; hence, a natural fear

results. One of the functions of religion is to alleviate some of this particular fear.

Loss of our lives before they have been fulfilled is
yet another fear we find in many individuals. All of
us have for ourselves a great goal, a great dream,
or a great sense of purpose. It is frightening to
think that something may happen to us before we
ever have an opportunity to accomplish that great
purpose.

Another fear, and one that, perhaps, for many
people, is the most common fear, is our fear of what
will become of our dependents when we die. We all
have the desire to make sure that our children are
raised, that our spouse is happy, that people who
are dependent on us can continue; it is very difficult for us to face our own potential death realizing
that these people must go on without us. We won-
der if we have fully enough provided for them in all
senses of the word. While this is a major fear,
another that relates quite closely is the fear that
we might not be missed at all. In fact, everyone
might continue quite well without us; our spouse
will find a new mate, our children will accept a new
parent, our employer will find someone to replace
us on the job. That sense of being replaced, of not
being needed, is a very frightening thought for
most people.

These, then, represent the most common fears of
death. How do people handle these fears? Edwin
Shneidman (1973) has suggested several types of

attitudes or intentions toward death. Some people show a great deal of acceptance toward death. They live life fully but always with a view toward the fact that it will end one day. Such people seem to savor every moment of life, getting something out of every experience. When death comes near, they don't want to let go of life, but they accept what must be.

Another type of person may simply acquiesce to death. They don't really care to think about it, and it does not motivate any of their behavior. Their attitude is one of simply saying, "Oh sure I'll die, but I don't really want to think about it."

A third type of response may be seen in people whose fear of death is so great that they don't want to have anything to do with any events related to death. They refuse to go to a funeral home, and certainly they would not visit a dying friend.

These are only some of the possible reactions people may have. Everyone responds differently, and our reactions and responses vary throughout the life span. For most individuals, the fear of death becomes greatest during the middle years of life. This is the time when we see our children able to function on their own. We are also at the peak of our profession and earnings, and everything seems to be going the way we want it to go. In the midst of this success, we suddenly ask ourselves, "What happens if it all ends now?" Death becomes the great interrupter, and in that sense, it is perhaps the most frightening. By contrast, as we move into old age, the fear of death subsides, and death may be seen as a friend rather than "the enemy."

Fears of the dying process are somewhat different. For many individuals, the fear of dying is far greater than the fear of death (Fulton, 1963). First and foremost in our fear of dying, we fear the pain associated with death. For many years, the phrase "death agony" became the conception most people had of what dying must be like. In reality, there is very little reason today for an individual to die in pain. We have medications that can keep patients relatively pain-free and yet alert so that they are able to say their goodbyes and do those things that are so important for them to do. In addition to medication, one's attitude can change the degree of pain experienced. Learning to meditate, using self-hypnosis, learning to think about other kinds of things can all be used to alleviate pain. It is important for us to make sure that dying people do not have to experience physical pain.

The second fear related to the dying process is that of being a burden. We struggle in our early years of life to become independent, functioning people. Finally, as we emerge from adolescence and complete our education, we step out into the world on our own. There is something in us that rebels against our ever having to be a burden on someone else or for someone else to have to provide for us. However, when we face dying, frequently because of the debilitations of the illnesses themselves, we find ourselves once again dependent on other people—people to take care of us physically, emotionally, and perhaps financially. Most of us resist very strongly this notion of being a burden. We may, for example, worry about how the bills will be paid, if we are, in fact, dying. Dying is an expensive process. Will the family be burdened with all of those bills? If a person is in an institution, will the family be burdened in the sense of having to spend hours and hours, day after day, at the institution, taking them away from friends and activities and the outside world? If the patient goes home to die under a hospice program, does that mean that it would be less possible for the children to have their friends come to visit? Will people have to tiptoe around the house so as not to disturb the individual and to make sure that he or she gets the necessary rest? The whole dying process becomes very disruptive and anxiety-producing.

In talking with patients in nursing homes—elderly patients—one of the things they often say is, "I just don't want to be a burden on someone." For this reason, many of us, when we contemplate death, think that our preference would be for a quick death as opposed to something that would produce not only pain but also give that sense of being a burden to others.

The third and major fear of the dying process is that of the indignities of death. Because of being categorized as either terminal or having a life-threatening illness, many people find themselves dependent on others in terms of being told how to behave. This often means giving up certain freedoms and a sense of responsibility to self. A patient in a hospital may well be told when to go to sleep, when to wake up, and quite often, what to do when awake. This can be extremely frustrating to one's sense of dignity. A patient diagnosed as having only a short time to live and finding himself on a salt-free, low-carbohydrate diet has great difficulty understanding why this is necessary when it is common knowledge that even prisoners on death row are allowed to pick anything they want to eat for their last meal. Sterile surroundings, unfamiliar routines, and visitor restrictions all promote a nightmare-like, unreal world for a terminal patient. What happens to one's sense of personal dignity when one's natural bodily functions fail or one has to be helped and watched in the bathroom while carrying out previously private rituals? What happens to personal dignity when friends and family alike come to visit and confront a patient with tubes extruding from almost every body cavity? It is not difficult to understand why, for many people, indignity becomes the greatest fear of all. The unfortunate reality is that this need not be. Institutional settings can be adapted to accommodate better the specific needs and desires of the dying patient and to remove much of that fear of the dying process.

There are other fears, perhaps not as significant, of the dying process, but fears nonetheless. One of these is loneliness—the fact that, because people have such fears of death in general, they will stay away from a person during the dying process, and he or she will be isolated from other human beings and not have the opportunity to have the contact with them that he or she would like to have. Some people may fear that they will die too quickly in the process before they can finish those things they find important. There may even be a fear in some people that they can't talk with others because others are so uncomfortable with what is happening that they don't want to talk about what the patient is feeling and thinking and what it is like to face death. Some people may even feel a sense of humiliation and regression that, as they are dying, they will regress to an earlier level of behavior or will become frightened and will show themselves cowards in the face of death.

Most of these fears can be overcome. In death, and in the dying process, people do remain valued people. Even after death, our lives continue through our children, through the work we have done, through the memories of those around us.

There is another set of fears that relate to the dying process. These are the fears not of the dying person but rather the fears of those of us who confront dying people—fears that, perhaps, keep us from being willing to spend time with dying individuals. Part of the fear of being around dying people may well be the fact that in those persons we "see" people close to us. This same thing, incidentally, carries through into the grief process. Very often, married women seem to disavow their relationships with other women who were once friends and who now are widows because of the frightening aspect of seeing in the widow the fact that one day they too may be alone. For some of us that fear goes a little bit further in the sense that in the dying patient we see ourselves. One day, we too will be in that position. One day, we too will be facing death, and it is difficult for us to face that reality any more than is necessary.

Another major part of our fear of dying people is the fact that we lack the knowledge of what to say to them. If one should walk into the room of a dying patient, a friend whom we know is dying and who knows himself that he is dying, what should we say to him? The answer is very simple. We start with, "Hello," followed quickly by, "How are you?" There is one important catch in this simple approach. If we ask, "How are you?" we must be prepared for the answer. Dying patients are honest. They will tell us exactly how they are. When they are finished, we can't simply say, "That's nice," and walk away. We must be ready to deal with the feelings, the emotions, the angers, the frustrations, and the fears those patients have. We must also be willing to stay and to take our time with them, to provide them with the support they need. Talk to dying patients, ask them questions, deal with their fears; it is difficult to do this but ultimately very rewarding to both people involved.

If these, then, are the most common fears of dying, how do we deal with them? How do we confront them in our daily lives? To a large extent, we confront our fears by simply denying death, by not confronting the reality which produces the fear. There are several ways in which death is denied. In some instances, it is denied by simply being ignored as totally as possible. When we talk about buying insurance, for example, we buy life insurance, not death insurance. The very knowledge of what it is we are purchasing would increase our fear, so we ignore it. We ignore death by burying the obituaries in the second section or on the last page of the newspaper. Only if a major world figure or community figure dies, do we see it up front, up close. Funeral homes are often built to look like houses, beautiful homes, to allow us to deny that death even happens.

Another way in which we deal with our fear of death is not to deny death but to deny the harshness of death. The euphemisms we use are good examples of this: expire, depart, pass away, pass on, eternal sleep. All of these are words used to soften the blow of death. In reality, however, these words do more harm than good. They give us a way

to deny something that is a part of life, and consequently little is accomplished in the denial itself. It
often becomes clear in working with grieving individuals that part of getting the grief work moving
is to make people face the full reality, the harshness that death implies. That is not easy. Death is
painful. Death hurts. However, the reality must be
confronted.

Another way in which we show death denial is to
make death very commonplace. If, during a war,
death exists on the fronts of newspapers every day,
and on the fronts of all the news magazines, very
quickly we become almost callous to it. We simply
skip over it as if nothing happened. The more
commonplace it becomes, the easier it becomes to
ignore. This may even exist as a result of shows on
television where we see individual after individual
shot and killed; pretty soon we stop thinking about
it.

For some people, rather than trying to deny
death, their attempt is to face it. Naturally, there
are different ways in which people find an appropriate sense of being able to face death in their
lives. For some people, we find that they develop a
pre-nostalgia to personal death. That is, periodically, they think of their own death; the thought
brings forth a sorrowing experience. Perhaps that
is a very appropriate, normal kind of response to
see in one. It may exist both in terms of thinking of
their own death or the potential death of some

friend or loved one. Some people deal with death by an attempt to overcome it. We overcome death, in part, by procreation, by having children, by having our names carried on in our children for generations to come. We overcome death by the money we give to organizations or charities that bear our name; hence the name and memory will live long after we die. During the Bicentennial era, a book was published listing notable Americans of the Bicentennial era. When people received information about the book and the opportunity to be listed in the book, the point was made that people will be able to look in this book years from then and see who a person was. This is what we do with *Who Was Who* and similar kinds of volumes. We all look for ways to become immortal.

Finally, some people deal with their death and face it with an attitude of participation: "I've done all I can to fight death. It is going to happen and I want to experience it to the fullest." Sometimes we even find patients who, when given the opportunity to be asleep and pain free at the moment of death, choose instead to be a part of their death experience. These people have very probably chosen all their lives to experience everything to the fullest degree possible and see no reason why this should not also extend to their deaths.

Assuming that all of us have the fears we've talked about, how then can we best cope with them? Only by recognizing that death is something that affects all of us. All of us, many times in our lives, will experience the death of someone close to us—someone with whom it is difficult to part. However, we learn over time that memories stay with us and that people do live on through our lives and in the memories they have given us. So, too, as we think of our own death, difficult as that may be, we must learn to recognize the fact that death comes to all of us sooner or later. All of our scheming, all of our kicking—none of these things can stop it.

Someone wrote that perhaps the screaming and crying that occurs during the birth process on the part of the newborn baby represents an unwillingness to come into this world. Yet, the child does come into this world and, despite whatever else it may find, finds joy in life. Could it be that our screaming and kicking to avoid leaving this life represents the same thing and that at the end of our dying process we too may find something of value and joy waiting for us?

REFERENCES AND/OR ADDITIONAL READINGS

Fulton, R. L. (1963). *The sacred and the secular: Attitudes of the American public toward death.* Milwaukee: Buffin.

Means, M. H. (1936). Fears of one thousand college women. *Journal of Abnormal and Social Psychology, 31,* 291-311.

Schneidman, E. S. (1973). *Deaths of man.* New York: Quadrangle Books.

Explaining Death To Children

If you are the parent or friend of a child who is afraid to talk with the child about death, you are not alone. Most of us hesitate to talk about death, particularly with young people, but death is a fact of life. We must learn that, despite our adult anxieties surrounding death, we still cannot shield children from death-related experiences. We must somehow give them permission to talk about death and their feelings about death. By taking time to talk with our children about death, we can discover what it is they know and don't know. We may even learn something about their misconceptions, their fears, and their worries. Only by doing this are we able to help them in trying to understand the reality of death. Only then are we able to provide the comfort and understanding that children may need as they deal with the reality of death.

In the best of all possible worlds, we would explain death to a child at an early age in a normal, matter-of-fact fashion. However, most of the time, this simply does not happen. A child experiences the death of a pet. Rather than allowing the child to understand what death and loss feel like, the tendency on the part of many parents is to replace the pet immediately, sometimes without telling the child the original pet has died. These parents are discounting their child's intelligence if they truly believe one black and white kitten is exactly like another black and white kitten. Perhaps a parent tells a child that the pet has run away, but they'll get the child another one. Sometimes, even if a parent is honest and indicates that a pet has died, they immediately destroy that moment of loss by quickly saying, "But don't worry. We can get another." Consequently, it is not surprising to contemplate how many children, when they discover that a parent or close relative has died, might begin to think, "Oh, but we can get another."

What is it that children do understand about death? Obviously, their understanding will vary with their developmental age. Generally, we can recognize a series of stages, first identified by Marie Nagy (1948).

For the first four or five years of life, a child really does not understand death as being final. For young infants, who are very dependent on their mothers, they are only beginning in the most rudimentary way to become aware of being separate persons. They are, nonetheless, acutely aware of separation from their mothers. As they near the age of four or five, their conception of death is simply one of going away: people go away and people come back. Death is temporary and sometimes seen as a state of sleep; nothing seems to give it a sense of reality.

Young children also engage in a great deal of "magical thinking." Consequently, the line between fact and fantasy may not be a clear one.

Many children may, at times, feel some sense of responsibility for the death of a loved one. It is not unusual, in the lives of all young children, to have experienced anger directed toward a parent and to follow that anger by thinking or saying, "I wish you'd go away and never come back." What happens, then, to the young child who has felt or expressed this sentiment only to discover shortly thereafter that Daddy or Mommy has indeed died and will never come back? We need to be more aware of children's thinking to avoid creating or fostering undeserved guilt.

Children around age five are very curious about death. They ask a lot of questions about heaven, angels, God, and burials: "What does it mean to be dead?" They have some awareness of death, but their concept of what death is all about is very immature.

From the ages of five to nine, children move into a different mode of thinking. Suddenly, they become aware that death is final—that when one dies he or she does not come back. Children also tend to spend a lot of time with personifications of death. Death is seen as the boogeyman, the skeleton, the ghost. While they do accept the fact of death, children also believe it certainly won't happen to them. They demonstrate a morbid interest in things related to death. For children who find a dead bird and bury it in the back yard, it is not unusual to find them, a few days later, digging up the bird to find out what has happened to it. Again, a natural part of learning about death is death play. Also, for many children up to around age nine, most of their understanding about death is in terms of violence and punishment. Death takes place in violent ways. Death is a form of punishment for acts committed.

Finally, also around age nine, children progress to a third stage where they develop a clear understanding not only that death is final, but also that it is natural, inevitable, and universal. All those around them will die. They, too, will die someday. Nothing prevents death, and so for the first time, most children have a fairly comprehensive and clear picture of what death is all about.

In order for children to progress through these developmental stages, and to come to an understanding and recognition of what death is all about, they need appropriate teaching. However, in most cases, children's exposure to death does not come from honest discussion with their parents or other significant adults; rather they gather their perceptions from other kinds of stimulii in their environment. One of the earliest conceptions of death for children comes out of nursery rhymes. Unfortunately, death, when it is shown, is reversible in nursery rhymes and fairy tales. There is an old version of Humpty-Dumpty that reads:

"Humpty-Dumpty sat on a wall.
At three o'clock he had a great fall.

The king set all the clocks back to two,
Now scrambled Humpty's as good as new."
See? There is no death. According to that nursery rhyme, death can always be corrected. In one of the versions of Little Red Riding Hood, the wolf eats grandmother, but when the woodsman comes along, he splits the wolf open and grandmother pops out again. Death isn't real. Death doesn't happen. Children see conceptions of presumed death in cartoons on television. If we watch a cartoon such as the Roadrunner and Wiley Coyote, we see Wiley Coyote constantly plotting new ways to get Roadrunner, but each time it backfires, and Wiley Coyote gets blown up or falls off a five thousand foot cliff. However, he's always back in the next scene. The portrayal of death is not real. Nothing dies in this make-believe environment. If these are the only things to which children are exposed, then they begin to get a very incorrect attitude and view of death. Some research has indicated that, by the time young people have reached the age of fifteen, they have probably seen programming on television in which over thirteen thousand people have died violently, but always death occurs in a world of make-believe.

What can we do to help children to understand when someone dies? How can we explain it to them? Probably the best thing we can do is to avoid doing things which give them misconceptions about death. For example, telling white lies to children simply doesn't work. Even a child as young as two years old doesn't really believe them when we say them. We will say something such as, "Grandmother has gone to eternal sleep," and then we are surprised when the child either develops insomnia or feels very bad because he or she didn't say goodnight when grandmother went to sleep. In another instance, we might say to a child, "God took your Father," and again we are surprised when the child becomes very angry with God:

"Why did God take my Father from me?"

"Well, He took him because He loved him."

"Oh. Doesn't He love me? He didn't take me."

"Well of course He loves you, but He needed your father."

"Didn't He understand that I need him too?"

As adults we understand what we mean by such explanations, but children do not. At young ages, children accept things literally as presented. Young children's thinking has not yet developed to the point that they are able to deal with the abstract nature of such explanations. Sometimes we equate death with travel or a long journey. Then one day we come home and say to our children that we have to go on a long trip, and the children immediately equate that with the fact that people who were sent on a trip before never returned. Sometimes we say to a child that a person died because he or she became very sick. Then, of course, the day comes when the child has a fever and we say, "I'm sorry but you can't go to school today because you're very sick." The problem is that we understand what we are saying, but the child takes us literally and relates it to what he may have been told earlier. What can we say, then, in a positive way? It is important to recognize that there is no simple answer in explaining death to a child. To a large extent, we will accomplish the most if we let the child lead us. You see, children know what they want to know. They know how much they are able to understand. So the guidelines for explaining death to children are fivefold:

1. Be accepting. Any death-related questions asked by a child, if asked in an honest, serious way, deserve an honest, serious answer. It is important, even though we may find the question silly or meaningless, that somehow we recognize that, for the child, it is an important question. A colleague of mine talks about a child who expressed a great sense of relief when he went to a funeral home to see his grandfather. Everyone wondered why he felt so relieved. He explained, "Because he has his head." The child had constantly heard everyone refer to 'the body' at the funeral home; nothing had been said about the head. This example points out the need for us to be very specific in what we tell a child and to verify the child's perception of what we have said.

2. Be honest. Never try to give a child an answer

that you yourself would not believe and accept. Children see through us. Children know how we respond to things. To give a child an explanation of death because we think it's the right thing to do, when we ourselves don't believe it, is not doing the child any good. It is only making the situation worse. In fact, if we lie to children, it is very possible that the children will distrust anything we explain to them from that point on; it is likely that children will really not believe us in terms of what we do.

3. Be straight forward. Try to answer the question as simply as possible and then stop. If the child wants more information, he will ask. There was an old television show in which a young child asked his father, "Daddy, where did I come from?" With great anxiety, the father went through a lengthy explanation of the birth process, and when it was finished, the child's response was, "Oh. Billy came from Buffalo. I thought maybe I did, too." We have to be careful to know exactly what children are asking us. Children know their own limits. Ideally, we provide them with an answer to the basic question asked and then stop. In most cases, the child will accept our answer, go away, and think about it for some time; perhaps several days or weeks later the child will come back and ask the next part of the question. Handled this way, the situation is less anxiety-ridden for everyone

concerned.

4. Don't lecture a child. It is all too tempting when we sit down to talk about some issue like death to turn it into the lesson of the day or to try to make some major points or moralize. Death deserves better than that. Children need to learn morals, and sometimes a point has to be made, but death is an emotional experience, and lectures simply don't suffice in terms of explaining this reality to a child.

5. Don't be afraid to say you don't know, when, in truth, you don't know. One has to be careful with this because sometimes we are so uncomfortable with something that we use it as a cop-out. It seems easier to say to the child, "I don't know about that," rather than face up to the realities of the child's question. It is all right to say you don't know if you honestly don't, but it might be very useful, particularly in situations surrounding death, to add that, "Together maybe we can find an answer." This sort of response provides the child with much more encouragement and much more support from the adult.

In addition to these guidelines for explaining death, there frequently are more practical concerns which must be dealt with. An issue that often arises when a death occurs is how much involvement to provide for the child during the days immediately following a death in the family. More and more we are learning that children need to be a part of the entire death experience. Today we know that it is not a good idea to send the children away to stay with some relatives until things get back to normal. That doesn't allow children to be a part of the whole family at that time, nor does it allow them their opportunity to mourn.

Should a child attend a funeral? In most cases, it is to be strongly recommended. We know, today, that funerals do not seem to do any damage to children. Rather, they help to draw a child closer to the family as a whole. However, children should not be forced to participate in something of which they do not wish to be a part. We must take time to explain to a child what might occur and what is involved in going to a funeral home and then provide them as much encouragement as possible to join the family, but they must never be forced. If, after our explanations and discussions, the child's choice is, "I do not want to go," then we must accept that decision. However, we must also find other ways in which the child could still be a part of what is going on at the time of the death. We might say to the child, for example, "All right, we are going to the funeral home and will be gone for a while, but there are probably going to be some people who come by the house to drop off food, or somebody may call. Would you stay here and take the phone calls or remember who brought food to us?" This is simply another way for the child to be a part of the funeral process, since that too is part of the ritual that surrounds death in our culture.

For the child who chooses not to go to the funeral home, to the viewing, or to the cemetery, we might also offer the opportunity to do something later. We might say to the child, "In a few weeks I need to go to the cemetery to see about the marker they are going to put on Grandad's grave. If you'd like, you can come with me then." Anytime children shut a door on involvement with death, on their chance to say their goodbyes, then we need to open some other door and to provide them with another opportunity so that at some future point they will not feel as though there is no more opportunity or chance to say goodbye.

Children need the experience of mourning and the funeral is one way in which that mourning can occur naturally. For children who do not go to the funeral home, it is important that we let them see how people mourn. There is nothing wrong with children discovering that their parents can cry. In many cases, it helps children to understand that tears are a part of being human. It is important for children who visit the funeral home that we watch that nobody puts them into an untenable position. We sometimes say to a child, "You're the man of the family now." This is a terrible responsibility to place on a child, and it denies him his opportunity to feel his grief. We might even say to a child, "Now there, big boys don't cry," almost teaching them that tears are wrong. Children have a need to be allowed to express their emotions just as much as adults.

Some of the needs of children which should be kept in mind would include the following:

1. Children need to learn how to mourn, i.e., to be able to go through the process, giving up the feelings that they have invested in some person or pet. They must realize that, despite the loss they may feel, they have to pick up and go on with their living. They need to understand that part of the mourning process is remembering to hold on to the memories of the person or pet who died. They need to know, as part of the mourning process, that it is normal and acceptable to feel anger: anger because somebody was responsible, anger because of being left behind, anger at being forced to feel unbearable loneliness.

2. We need to make sure that children have the opportunity to mourn over small losses — for example, the death of a pet — in order to deal better with larger losses. As adults, we often minimize the effect of a death. One of the techniques that is sometimes used in dealing with children is doll play — dolls that represent family members. Doll play allows the therapist a view of the family relationships from the standpoint of the particular child, but it also allows the child an unthreatening opportunity

to express and demonstrate those relationships. Several years ago a psychologist was working with a young child whose mother was terminally ill. The child was playing with the mother doll, mother of course being the one who was dying. Suddenly the child picked up the doll, walked out of the room, down the hall and into the bathroom where he proceeded to put the doll into the toilet and flush it away. The child finally explained, after some very in-depth questioning, that not too long before, his pet goldfish had died, and his parents had explained to him that all you do is flush it down the toilet. By minimizing that loss the parents had taught the child that loss doesn't hurt; loss is something we get over quickly. As a result, that was the only frame of reference within which the child was able to deal with the impending death of his mother. Children need to mourn those small losses in order to be able to deal more appropriately with closer, more critical losses.

3. Children need to be informed about death. We sometimes try to hide the fact that a death has occurred; for example, a grandparent who lives halfway across the country has died, and it is decided that since nobody from the household is going to the funeral, the children won't be told about the death. However, since the family will still be upset over the death, and children will

sense that something is wrong, by not being honest with children we will only confuse them about the source of our natural emotions. They need that honesty from us in order to avoid confusion, misconception, and the lack of development of very natural emotions.

4. Children need to understand the finality of death. For that reason, it is important that we not use fairy tale language, that we not use the euphemisms of "passing away," or "went away," or "gone to sleep," because none of these phrases imply things that are permanent. Death is a permanent loss. It is final. People who have died do not come back. It is important for children to know that they will not see the person or pet again here on earth.

5. Children need to say goodbye to the deceased. Hopefully, this can be accomplished by viewing at the funeral home, but if not, perhaps a private ritual in the home can be arranged in which the children can take part.

6. Children need opportunities to work out their feelings and to deal with their perceptions of death. One of the best ways in which we can allow children to experience the feelings of death is by exposing them to reading material that can be helpful. There are many good books available today for young children which can help them to have a better conception of death: *The Tenth Good Thing About Barney* (Viorst,

1971), *The Magic Moth* (Lee, 1972), *Annie and the Old One* (Miles, 1971), *The Dead Bird* (Brown, 1965), *My Grandpa Died Today* (Fassler, 1971), and *A Taste of Blackberries* (Smith, 1973). These are but a few of the many books that are on the market that deal with death in honest, realistic ways and do so at a level that even a young child can understand.

7. Children need reassurance that their parents will take care of them, and they need to deal with the potential loss of another significant other. For a child whose father has died, it is not helpful for the mother to say to the child, "Now don't worry, I'm not going to die and leave you." That amounts to representing some sense of certainty that none of us has. Rather, it would be important to have a conversation with the child, saying, among other things, "Daddy did not want to leave us, and certainly I don't want to leave you and I don't plan to die soon, but if something should happen to me, you will be taken care of." Then we can go on to explain to the child how that will happen. Young children are egocentric; they are very concerned about themselves and their security. We need to make sure that there is that sense of security for them.

8. Children need to understand that, despite the fact that someone has died — perhaps a young person, that most people do grow up and live

long lives and become old. This is not to create a false picture for children but simply to help them to understand that, although death sometimes happens in unusual ways, most of us will live to be old.

9. It is important that children be allowed to show their feelings, to become angry, to cry, to laugh — whatever is appropriate for them. We should empathize with their feelings, and certainly we should not take their feelings away from them. We must recognize that children will often mourn in their own way. For a young boy who comes home from school one day and discovers that his father has died unexpectedly, his response may be to go to his room, and then an hour or two later he may come down and announce that he is going fishing. We may not understand this response, and it may take us by surprise, but in reality it may be that the child is doing something that reminds him most of his father. On the other hand, a child may wish to engage in some seemingly unrelated activity: "May I go roller skating?" The reality is that for some children, this seemingly unrelated and inappropriate activity may be their way of handling their grief. Children need the opportunity to find what works best for them, just as adults need to find what works best for them.

Although the discussion to this point has been about young children, a few comments about adolescents seem in order. Adolescents have a great deal of difficulty dealing with death. Granted that by the time individuals reach adolescence they have developed a fairly mature concept of death, many teenagers really deny death. Much of the seemingly self-destructive behavior we see in adolescents — drug abuse, failure to follow medical advice, attempts at or discussions of suicide — may well be related to teenagers' inability to accept the fact that death is final. It also may represent their feeling of invulnerability to death (McCandless, 1970). Teenagers also have difficulty with their grief process because they are less likely to talk about their feelings. It is important to make teenagers aware of the availability of other adults, people who will listen to them when they discover that they are not comfortable opening up about this topic with their own parents.

How can we best summarize all this? Communicating about death, just as any kind of communication, is easier when children feel that they have permission to talk about it and when they believe that we are interested in what they have to say and in the questions they ask. Every child is different. How we discuss death with a child depends on the child's age, the child's experiences, and the child's needs. Very young children are only capable of absorbing a small amount of information at a time. The responses we give them and their questions about death should be simple and repeated, perhaps for a period of time, until they come to a recognition of what we are saying. Children often feel angry and guilty when someone close to them dies. They need to receive from us reassurances that they are loved and cared for and that the relationship they had with the dead person was a good one. Children need a long period of time to grieve. For a child, grief may last for five or ten years. A deeply felt loss will go on and on from the time children are very young until they are in their adolescence. They need from us support and an understanding that their feelings will come up again and again over the years.

No matter what we do, it is important to remember that words don't make the difference. It is our behaviors that do make a difference. You may be awkward and inarticulate as you try to explain death to children, but the important thing is the way in which you behave. They must have a sense of our sincerity in trying, a sense of reassurance that they receive from us. Finally, it is important to remember that children can be very therapeutic for us as adults if we will let them. Children frequently have a much easier time expressing their emotions, and in that sense, sometimes a child, more than any of our adult friends, can give us opportunities to express our true feelings. When it comes to a death, truth and honesty are the most important factors in bringing any person — child or adult — to a full realization of the loss which they have suffered and a full resolution to the grief they inevitably experience.

REFERENCES AND/OR ADDITIONAL READINGS

Anthony, S. (1972). *The discovery of death in childhood and after.* New York Basic Books.

Blueband-Langner, M. (1978). *The private worlds of dying children.* Princeton, New Jersey: Princeton University Press.

Brown, M. W. (1965). *The dead bird.* Glenview, Illinois: Scott.

Fassler, J. (1971). *My grandpa died today.* New York: Behavioral Publications.

Grollman, E. A. (1967). *Explaining death to children.* Boston: Beacon Press.

Lee, V. (1972). *The magic moth.* New York: Seabury.

Lenelto, R. (1980). *Children's conceptions of death.* New York: Springer.

LeShan, E. (1976). *Learning to say goodby: When a parent dies.* New York: Macmillan.

McCanless, B. R. *Adolescents — behavior and development.* Hinsdale, Illinois: Dryden Press.

Miles, M. (1971). *Annie and the old one*. Boston: Little, Brown.

Nagy, M. (1948). The child's theories concerning death. *The Journal of Genetic Psychology, 73*, 3-27.

Smith, D. B. (1973). *A taste of blackberries*. New York: Crowell.

Viorst, J. (1971). *The tenth good thing about Barney*. New York: Atheneum.

Death And The Health Care Professional

As our society has undergone changes, we have developed a death system that relies on a group of professionals. We have turned over virtually all aspects of dying to these professionals. In a broad sense, they can be considered a group of health care professionals, although in a more traditional sense we would not consider them all involved in health care, per se. Who are these professionals? How do they deal with death in our society?

One of the first health care professionals we can identify in our death system is the physician. The physician often has a very difficult time with death. In medical school training today, the emphasis is, as it should be, on saving lives. This emphasis, however, often develops in our physicians a totally objective and scientific approach to patients. Thus, physicians will do everything in their power to promote health and to maintain the lives of their patients. However, as will happen in all cases, sooner or later, patients will die. There comes a time when there is nothing more that can be done for certain patients from a medical standpoint. It is at this point that physicians often fail patients. This failure is seen in their lack of ability to maintain a contact with the patient, to provide now for their needs in dying as opposed to their needs in living. As physicians see patients' health deteriorating to a point where nothing more can be done medically, their attitude becomes one of failure. It is unfortunate that physicians cannot recognize that they truly have done all they can, medically, for a patient, but, inevitably, death will still come. At this point, our physicians need to learn to maintain their relationship with the patient but to change their goals from goals of cure to simply goals of care. What they can continue to provide for patients, as the patients experience dying, is to remain close to them — warm, caring, and personable. They must recognize the patient's need for truth and understanding. They need to see that the patient maintains the control over his own life and to do all they can to promote that sense of control. Following a death, the physician needs to be able to relate to the family, to care for some of the needs of those survivors who now become the "patients."

A second health care professional we can identify is the nurse. Nurses have, in most instances, far more day-to-day contact with the patient than does the physician. Thus, it is very likely that they will become more emotionally attached to the patient than will the physician. Nurses often find themselves in a unique position, namely that of dealing with many of the emotional needs of the dying patient. Patients will frequently confide to nurses more about their feelings than they will to their own families. Nurses do an outstanding job of caring for their patients. They, too, however, need to recognize the limits of medical knowledge and to accept the fact that at some point patients will still die. They can, however, in the dying process, continue to care for their patients and to help meet the specific emotional needs that the patients have for contact and conversation.

The third group of professionals in our death system is the clergy, those individuals of all faiths who are recognized as spiritual leaders. The clergy, too, are in a unique position to meet many of the specific needs of the dying patient, but often they fail to do so, perhaps, because, as so many other specialists, they fail to recognize that they are human beings first and professionals second. Consequently, although their task may be to deal with the spiritual needs of a patient, they can clearly do more than simply provide spiritual comfort. All too often, however, clergy, because of their professionalism and their special language and attire, set themselves apart from the patients for whom they are caring. Patients see them in an almost businesslike attitude encompassing rituals and not necessarily always in the caring role. Many clergy, obviously, are successful in caring for dying patients, but many need to develop a more personal way of caring for dying patients.

A fourth person we can identify in this complex of professionals in the death system is the funeral director. Funeral directors frequently come under a great deal of criticism from others, namely in terms of the great expense of funerals and the attitudes they may have. It is interesting to note that, in talking to bereaved individuals, they frequently identify the funeral director as the person who has been the most helpful to them, the one who provided the most comfort and support, far beyond what was expected (Fulton, 1979). Despite that support, some funeral directors fail to provide some of the needs in the death system. The funeral director's main contact in not with the patient but with the family. In that respect, they become a primary source of comfort. It is important that, although the funeral director should maintain a business relationship with a client and meet those specific needs associated with funerals, they too recognize that they are human beings and that they need to disassociate themselves from the uniforms of their trade and the badges of the serious face and simply represent themselves to families as one caring human being to another.

The last professional that we frequently associate with our death system would be the mental health specialist: the psychologist, psychiatrist, counselor or social worker who is often called upon either to work with a family following a death or perhaps with a patient and the family prior to the death. Of all the professionals, this group frequently does the poorest job in the death field, perhaps because for so long they have been able to see death-related issues as removed from their domain. The counseling profession is one dedicated to helping people to adjust and to change. We cannot change the fact that a person is dying, but we can alter people's attitudes. We can help them to cope with what is happening, but we cannot change the situation for them. Consequently, these professionals have often remained divorced from the death system. Today, we find very few counselors who have the special degree of training necessary to deal with death-related situations. We cannot always take basic counseling skills and apply them to patient care or to grief work. Our training of counselors often necessitates em-phasizing to them that they should not become too personally involved with the individuals with whom they are working. However, in working with dying patients and grieving individuals, that is almost impossible. We do become involved because of the fact that these people need to see a caring other. Consequently, we need to provide a better understanding on the part of mental health spe-cialists as to their role in the death process.

A final observation about professionals should be made. Any professional who works around death on a continual basis cannot help but be affected by it. Consequently, we must provide op-portunities for the professional to deal with his or her own needs. We speak often of "burn-out," the idea that the continued strain and involvement of work may cause ineffectiveness and loss of enthusiasm. Clearly, working with death and dying is stressful. Nevertheless, if professionals make room for their own needs and learn to balance work and personal involvement with caring for themselves, burn-out need not occur. Rather, they will be able to continue providing the level of care they always have.

Our death system is changing. The role of the professional is changing. What we must begin to do is to educate our professionals more fully in order for them to work with the needs of dying people, to help them to understand the special kinds of problems that death brings to us, and through that training, to make them better able to deal and cope with those persons reaching out for their help.

REFERENCES AND/OR ADDITIONAL READINGS

Fulton, R. (1979). Death and the funeral in contemporary society. In H. Wass (Ed.), *Dying: Facing the facts*. Washington, D.C.: Hemisphere.

Kasper, A.M. (1965). The doctor and death. In H. Feifel (Ed). *The meaning of death*. New York: McGraw-Hill.

Kastenbaum, R. (1963). The reluctant therapist. *Geriatrics, 18,* 296-301.

Kastenbaum, R. & Aisenberg, R. (1972). *The psychology of death*. New York: Springer.

Care of the Dying Patient

Historically, care of the dying patient was a family function. When individuals neared the ends of their lives, either through specific illness or simple advancement of age, they remained in their own homes to be cared for by their families. It would be these same loved ones who would surround the bed, as death approached, enabling patients to maintain some control at the end of life and giving them enough time to say their good-byes.

With medical advancement and the rapid technology accompanying it, the dying were removed from the home environment and placed into institutional settings to be cared for by well-trained and well-intentioned specialists. Yet, these well-meaning professionals were not the people to whom the patient had been close in life, and as death neared, patients would often find themselves at the end of the hall in a room behind closed doors. Death would come among strangers and in a strange environment.

In the past fifteen years, there has developed a renewal of interest in the needs of the dying patient and the desire to understand better what can be done to make the patient as comfortable and as fulfilled as possible at the end of life. In 1969, Elisabeth Kubler-Ross published her classic book,

On Death and Dying. Although prior to this date there was an interest in the needs of the dying patient, it was this work that made people far more aware of that which patients would experience in their final days of life. Dr. Ross identified a series of five stages in those patients with whom she worked. These stages have come to be referred to as the stages of dying. Since 1969, much has been written, both supporting and questioning this stage concept. Nonetheless, the stages still provide us with a base from which to build. They provide for us a useful overview of what the patient may experience, and they are equally applicable to the family during the same process. It is important to recognize that the stages cannot be taken rigidly. In some patients, they may not occur in order. In other patients, some stages may never be manifested. Some individuals will die in one of the early stages; other individuals will experience a shift between the stages on a daily, if not hourly, basis. As we look at these stages, it is important to keep in mind that they represent reactions, not a hard and fast system. They do, however, give us an opportunity to study and understand these reactions that patients may have and, consequently, to determine what we, in turn, can do to be supportive of them at that time.

Denial is the first stage identified by Kubler-Ross. Denial represents that initial reaction of patients when first confronted with a life-threatening illness. It is a refusal to believe that this could be happening to them. The denial is often manifested by a trek from one specialist to another, to find someone who will provide a different diagnosis. Denial may also include questioning the credibility of the physician who provided the initial information. Denial is a healthy process; it is a defense mechanism. Denial provides patients with the opportunity to come to grips with the very real tragedy that is happening to them. It gives them the chance to deal with their new experience of a sense of isolation from the living world.

What do we do for patients who are experiencing denial? We allow them to deny. We really cannot take that denial away from them. Patients do not want to believe that this is happening to them. It is important that they recognize that there are those people available who will be willing to talk to them when they need to talk, but that for the time being, they will be allowed to react in their own way.

Given time, most patients move from a reaction of denial to one of anger. In the anger reaction, patients are no longer denying that this tragedy is happening to them, but rather they question why it should be happening to them. Why not some other individual? They begin to reflect back on their lives and on all the positive things they have done, reflecting on all the reasons they have to continue living; they decide that it is very unfair for this to be happening to them now. The reaction includes tremendous feelings of resentment and rage, anger that may be directed at the health care professional, at members of their families, at God, or at the world in general. The anger is very real because in each person they come in contact with they see someone who will go on living, and they know that their time is very limited.

In the anger stage it is very important that we do not desert patients. They need to be given the opportunity to have an outlet for their anger and their hostility. Granted, none of us likes to be around angry, hostile people, but if we can pause for a moment and understand where the anger is coming from, hopefully we will be able to deal with it and not desert the patient in this most difficult time.

Following anger, many patients will move on to a reaction of bargaining. They begin to recognize that the anger has accomplished nothing. If anything, it has simply driven people away from them, and it certainly has not changed the diagnosis. Hence, they try to go in an opposite direction, namely that of being on their best behavior. They think, "Perhaps if I'm good, I can gain more time by some kind of an agreement." So they begin to look for possible ways of extending their life expectency. They try to forestall the inevitable ending. They ask for one more opportunity to do things. They want to live through one more Christmas. They want to see one more child graduate from school. They want to be there for the christening of one more grandchild.

Sometimes bargains are struck with physicians: "If you can make me pain free for a couple of weeks so I can attend my granddaughter's graduation, then I'll go into the hospital and do anything you want me to do." Most often, however, the bargains are struck with God: "If you'll only let me live until next Christmas, I'll be good; I'll do good things."

It is interesting to note that bargaining works to a degree for many patients. Time and time again we find individuals who manage to live until that particular significant event occurs. Recognize, however, that most patients, if they make it that far, are not about to quit. One more event turns into another and another and another. We need to do anything we can to support the patient in this bargaining process, but clearly we cannot make guarantees beyond our control.

The fourth reaction we see in many patients is that of depression. Depression seems to take two forms. The first form of depression is that which we refer to as reactive depression. It is the depression which patients experience as the result of what is happening to them: their pain — physical and mental, the sense of losses that they are currently experiencing, perhaps some of their concerns over financial issues and care of their families. We can help a person with reactive depression sometimes by providing a pain medication that will not dull their senses or suggesting assistance related to financial worries or alternatives to family problems.

The second type of depression is different and is referred to as preparatory depression. Preparatory depression is a type of anticipatory grieving, in which individuals are grieving over the sense of loss of people and things significant to them, things that will no longer be theirs. We cannot take away preparatory depression. Indeed, we probably do not want to. It is an opportunity for patients to come to grips with what is happening to them and to prepare themselves for the inevitability of their own loss. That doesn't mean, however, that there is nothing we can do. We can provide our physical presence. We can provide quiet listening and understanding. Simply being with the patient, knowing what they are going through, with the total absence of words, can still do a great deal to help them to cope with this stage.

The last stage which Kubler-Ross identified was that of acceptance. Acceptance represents a coming to terms with what is happening without feeling good about it. This is the stage that follows the struggle of the denial and anger and bargaining and depression. It is not, however, a stage of resignation. It is, rather, a period of calm with some degree of sadness and a great deal of reflection. It is often during this time that the needs of the family become greater than the needs of the patient.

Throughout the five stages, the family experiences the stages as well as the patient, but in most instances, the family lags behind the patient. When a patient reaches a stage of acceptance, the family may still be engaged in a great deal of denial, anger, bargaining, or depression. With the stage of acceptance, patients begin their own disengagement from the world around them and may, from time to time, send the family away so that they can become used to going on with life without these people. However, the family often has a lot of difficulty in dealing with this kind of detachment, and they need support from others in understanding why the patient wants to have things happen in this manner. It is important to recognize that the stages suggested above do not occur in a predictable, neat order for all patients. Each person is an individual. Each person's dying is different. We cannot look upon stages so rigidly that we begin to expect things from our patients that may not be real to them. We cannot, and must not, direct our patients to move from one stage to the next. We can, however, facilitate those changes that are natural parts of their own reactions.

A woman in her early sixties had been in and out of the hospital several times in a three year period, twice for major surgery. Now she was once again in the hospital, terminally ill, diagnosed as having cancer of the throat. Her daughter was sitting by her bed and they had chatted quietly about nothing in particular for some time. Suddenly, the mother took her daughter's hand and said, "I'm not going to make it this time, am I?"

With tears welling in her eyes, the daughter answered simply, "No, Mom."

The two sat there holding hands in silence for quite a while. Then the mother spoke again: "I forgot what we were talking about."

Again, the daughter answered simply, "That's okay, Mom. When you're ready, you'll remember."

And again, they sat holding hands in silence. The next time the mother spoke, ten minutes later, it was to tell the daughter that she didn't want to die in the hospital; she wanted to go home but didn't know if the daughter could take care of her. The next morning the daughter took her mother home. Two weeks later the mother died, quietly, in her own bed, with her daughter sitting by her side, holding her hand.

This account illustrates two important points. First, the daughter did not push her mother nor deny her the truth for which she was asking. She simply helped her mother to deal with her dying in her own way. Secondly, it shows how quickly a person may move back and forth through the stages. They may take weeks or months, or, as in this case, only minutes. It would seem as though patients often manages to compress or expand the time in each stage to fill the time they have left even though no one can tell them how much time that will be.

Kubler-Ross suggests one other important concept to accompany these stages. This is the concept of hope. Throughout all the stages hope is present. No matter how far into acceptance of the diagnosis and of their terminality patients may have progressed, they will, in almost all cases, continue to maintain some hope for a cure, remission, or indeed, a miracle. Hope is positive. Hope gives patients something which helps to maintain their will to live. It gives them something that lets them go on with the treatments and lets them go on through each day of life. We must, however, be careful not to give patients unrealistic hopes which will drive them back into the early stages in the process. Unrealistic hope will not give them the very necessary opportunities to confront the situation as it now exists.

The issue of how much to tell dying patients about their illnesses and prognoses is one with which many of us deal either as families or as caregivers. Perhaps this concern would not be so great if we could come to realize that the majority of individuals are well aware of what is happening to them long before anyone tells them anything. We recognize in our own bodies when things are not functioning properly. We are aware that we are unable to do things we once could do. We know when we can no longer eat certain foods or keep foods down or move out of our beds. Thus, in a very real sense, it may be that we are telling patients nothing they do not already know. We find, however, that different situations arise from patient to patient, reflecting different degrees of knowledge of their illness.

In 1965, Glasser and Strauss suggested a series of awareness contexts that exist for patients dealing with terminal illness. These contexts can provide us with some guidelines as to the effects of providing or not providing information to patients. In some cases, we deal with what we can refer to as a closed awareness system. This is simply to say that the decision has been made by medical staff and family that it is best not to let patients know what is happening to them. This may be appropriate, in limited cases, where perhaps we are dealing with an individual who has suffered brain damage and would really not understand what was being said, but for most people, it will probably make for a difficult and unreal situation. When we choose not to inform patients of the diagnosis of their true condition, we are denying those patients the opportunity to have any kind of say in the way in which their lives end. We are denying the possibility of being able to deal with unfinished business, that is, an opportunity to talk to particular people, to complete particular tasks, to put their personal affairs in order, to maintain and mend relationships. These individuals may well die without ever having the opportunity to close their lives as they see fit. It often happens, also, that following the death of a patient, where this lack of honesty has existed, the grief process for the survivors is more difficult as well.

Sometimes we find patients in what we refer to as a suspected awareness context. In suspected awareness, it has, again, been decided not to let patients know their true condition, but because of the very nature of the things happening to them, patients begin to suspect. This creates some very difficult situations; over a period of time, patients will begin to test people, and they will ask questions of the nurses and other health care personnel and within their own families. These questions could concern how long will they be in the hospital, why they can't seem to eat as they once did, or why they are not putting on weight. Because we become uncomfortable with those questions and fear that we may give information away that we don't want to, we might have a tendency to stay away from the patient. We may opt not to have contact with them for fear of breaking down and providing them with information we don't want to tell them. Not only does this mean that patients die without clear knowledge, but in fact, there is a strain on the relationships that do exist for the patient and a lack of opportunity to communicate.

A third situation which may arise is that of mutual pretense. In mutual pretense, everyone is aware of the diagnosis. The family understands, and the patient is aware; however, they have decided for themselves that it is best not to bring it up to the others involved. Hence, the family tries to pretend that the patient is probably not aware, and they are certainly not going to talk to them about it. The patient, similarly, decides that the strain would be too much on the family, and although he can deal with what is happening, he does not want to bring it up to them. This situation is better than the first two because at least the patient does know the truth and is able to do those things that he believes to be important. However, it still means that there is a lack of close, honest communication between the patient and those close to him.

The last context is that of an open system. In the open system, everyone is able to communicate freely about this knowledge. Consequently, patients are able to complete their lives as they wish, to say those things that are important to other people they care about, and to deal with the very real losses that are happening in their lives. The open system promotes communication. It promotes a greater degree of caring for the dying patient. In most death situations, these reactions become almost stages themselves. That is, initially, patients are usually unaware of what is happening, but over a period of time, they become aware until one day the information is honestly given to them. We can only hope that for most patients, or for the majority of patients, the open awareness arrives in time for them to complete their lives according to their wishes.

What then, can we do in caring for the dying patient? There is no simple formula. However, whether we are nurses, physicians, janitors, clergy, or significant family members of the dying patient, there are things we can do to make things easier both for them and for ourselves as well. First and foremost would be listening. All too often we stay away from dying patients because we simply are not sure of what to say to them. Most dying persons are not looking for words from us. Rather, they are looking for someone who will listen to their rantings and ravings, to their tears, to their hopes, and to their fears. That listening means that we become companions, caring friends to the patient, people who will not desert them, people who are available to them. Listening goes along with physical presence. Many times we can do a great deal for patients by simply sitting in their rooms with them for a period of time, no words passing between; yet, all the time, patients are clearly aware that we are there and that we are there because we want to be there and because we care.

Another thing that can be very helpful to the patient is physical touch. Sometimes, holding hands, placing an arm on the shoulder, or touching the forehead communicates more to a patient than any other act we might perform. It is, again, a way in which we show a patient that we care, that we cannot understand what it must be like for them, but that we want to help and care for them.

We can also deal with dying patients by accepting the fact that they are unique human beings. No two people die alike. Each person has his own way of dealing with this last tragedy of life. Consequently, we cannot impose our expectations on a dying patient, but rather we must deal with them on their own terms and in the way which they prefer.

Perhaps another way in which we can show and care for the patient is to recognize that there are no right and wrong emotions when it comes to death. Even in the tragedy of dying, there is a time and a place for laughter and smiles. All emotions are acceptable. We need to allow patients the opportunity to continue to be unique, functioning individuals and to show their emotions as long as they are living.

A final way in which we can help patients is in dealing with the pain they are experiencing. Dying brings to us both physical and psychological pain, and sometimes we cannot distinguish the two. We can help patients with their pain with medication. If we see that physical pain is not abating, we can change the dosage or recommend a change of medication. Not only can we medicate to relieve pain, but hopefully we can provide medication in order to prevent pain. However, we need to recognize that much of the pain is psychological; hence, other methods may assist in removing physical pain. Perhaps we can teach patients relaxation techniques, ways to deal with some of the emotional issues they are confronting and with some of the relationships that they must deal with; all of these may go a long way in assisting in the removal of pain. What all of these ideas represent is the simple truth that we must meet our patients on their terms, doing what they want, when they want.

A few words should be said about the needs of the family. When we are working with a dying patient, the family becomes our patient as well. Sometimes dying is more difficult for the family than for the patient. As suggested earlier, families go through the same kinds of reactions as patients do, but frequently it is a slower process, and hence, their problems may be more extreme. There are things that we can do, however, to assist them in the strain which they are experiencing, with the communication difficulties, with the changes that are occurring within the family structure. First, it is most important that families understand exactly what a patient is experiencing. By keeping them aware of what medications patients are taking, what changes in their condition are taking place, whether they have had a good night or a bad night, we make it easier for the family to recognize why the patient may be responding as they are. Families also need an opportunity to express their feelings. As the dying process continues, and prolongs itself in some cases, it becomes very difficult for some families, and sometimes their feelings may become that of wishing that the whole process were over. Yet there is guilt that accompanies that kind of feeling. So, families have feelings that they need an opportunity to talk about with someone, and we, as the caregivers, can provide that opportunity. Families need help in communicating with the dying patient. Sometimes they need to hear from others what they can do, what would make it easier. Finally, families need help with their grief. No matter how long an illness may have lasted, when death finally occurs, there is grief to be dealt with, and a family needs to know that at that time they will not be deserted because the job of the caregiver has finished. It is important to follow up our care of the patient with our care of the family, to spend some time with them following a death, to give them an opportunity to spend some time with the person after death, and perhaps, if at all possible, to do follow-up with the family weeks or months later with a phone call, something to indicate that we are thinking of them.

In the beginning of this chapter it was mentioned that care of the dying has undergone many changes from death at home to death at institutions. Today, health care professionals are reassessing the entire approach of care provided to dying patients. A discussion of care of the dying would not be complete without some mention of the role of the hospice today. The hospice movement started as an attempt to provide care for people who were facing a terminal illness. It has among its goals: doing everything possible to relieve pain and prevent pain; providing the opportunity wherever possible for patients to die at home or in environments more conducive to living; providing supportive care to both patient and family by providing time and opportunities for them to deal with other things in their lives; facilitating the family ties; and, in short, making it possible for patients to live as fully as possible for the time they have.

Much hospice care today takes place at home with the assistance of volunteers and professionals and lay persons. In some instances, hospice care is provided in a facility, either within an already existing hospital or in a free-standing facility. Regardless of its setting, its philosophy is the same, namely that of care of the dying patient.

Hospice has become a very important form of care for the dying patient. Clearly, it fulfills a need in our society. However, we must be careful over time that, out of our concern for changing the way in which we deal with dying patients, we do not create a new institution with its own unique problems. The best care we can provide for dying patients is to recognize that they are living patients. The only difference between the patients we care for and ourselves is that they have been provided with some time limit on their life expectancies. One day the patient we care for may well be ourselves. If we work now to improve the care of dying patients, if we do the best we can to help them, perhaps one day someone will be there to help us too.

REFERENCES AND/OR ADDITIONAL READINGS

Barton, D. (Ed.). (1977). *Dying and death: A clinical guide for caregivers.* Baltimore: Williams and Wilkins.

Glaser, B.G. & Strauss, A.L. (1965). *Awareness of dying.* Chicago: Aldine.

Hamilton, M.P. & Reid, H.F. (Eds.). (1980). *Hospice Handbook: A new way to care for the dying.* Grand Rapids, Michigan: William B. Erdmans.

Kubler-Ross, E. (1969). *On death and dying.* New York: Macmillan.

Stoddard, S. (1978). *The hospice movement: A better way to care for the dying.* New York: Random House.

The Rituals of Death

In our contemporary, technological society many of the rituals of the past have become unacceptable and discarded. This is true in many areas of life, but particularly so in terms of death. We are finding, as time goes by, that, without the continuation of some of these rituals, there is often little help for individuals as they begin the long grief process. Individuals who work with grieving people have recognized for some time the significance of having rites, rituals, and leave-taking ceremonies as something which can assist in the grief process. Traditionally, the main leave-taking ceremony of death has been that of the funeral. Funerals serve a variety of purposes. First and foremost, funerals give us an acceptable way of disposing of a body. More importantly, funerals serve as an aid in reorienting a survivor following the death of a loved one. It helps, in a sense, to define one's grief and to channel the emotions into a socially acceptable means of expression. Funerals also can serve as a public acknowledgement of death and provide an opportunity to bring a community of grievers together in support of each other and in recognition of the finite nature of life.

Over the years, funerals have been the recipients of continuing criticism. In Jessica Mitford's famous book, *The American Way of Death* (1963), much is made of the notion of a funeral as a barbaric ritual and as one which serves to extract a costly price from society. This is in contrast to the responses of individuals who have been through the grief process who frequently indicate that funeral directors and the funeral process were the most helpful aspects of learning to cope with deaths as they occurred (Glick, et al, 1974).

Funerals may take many forms. In some instances, funerals are conducted solely by the professionals, that is the funeral director and the minister. In more cases today, however, families are taking part in the funeral ritual and may, in fact, deliver part of the message of the funeral service. This is a return to practices which existed in the early 1900s.

Funerals represent but one of a variety of rituals that could accompany the death situation. In today's society, many people opt for a memorial service. This is particularly true where there has been a body donation to science or, perhaps, immediate cremation following death. In these cases there is no opportunity to have a body present for a traditional funeral service, and therefore, a service in memory is held some time following the death. Regardless of whether we choose the traditional funeral or a memorial service, the use of rituals is an important part of death. Rituals give us an opportunity to experience a rite of passage, a chance to say a final good-bye. It may be that rather than disbanding the rituals and ceremonies of death as we tend to do today, we may need to institute additional ceremonies. Could it be possible that in the days in which mourners were identified by black armbands and wreaths on the door that society provided more support for them? Were they able to identify more clearly their roles as grievers? Is it not also possible that religions which provide for specific markers, dates, and anniversaries do more good for grieving individuals?

Rituals and ceremonies are important. Ceremonies help to establish the fact of death as an emotional reality for both the bereaved person and the community as a whole. They are opportunities for others to offer their support. They give a chance for all to recognize the human side of life.

REFERENCES AND/OR ADDITIONAL READINGS

Fulton, R. (1979). Death and the funeral in contemporary society. In H. Wass (Ed.). *Dying: Facing the facts*. Washington, D.C.: Hemisphere.

Glick, I.O., Weiss, R.S. & Parkes, C.M. (1974). *The first year of bereavement*. New York: Wiley.

Mitford, J. (1963). *The American way of death*. New York: Simon and Schuster.

Morgan, E. (1980). *A manual of death education and simple burial (9th ed.)*. Burnsville, North Carolina: Celo Press.

Pine, V.R. (1975). Caretaker of the dead: The American funeral director. New York: Irvington Publishers.

Weisman, A. (1972). *On dying and denying*. New York: Behavioral Publications.

Aging

In our society, there is a continuing attitude that youth is such a lively time of existence; consequently, death is simply inappropriate and unnecessary. As we reach our adult years, we behave almost as if death grants us some special immunity: we will not have to deal with our own death for a long time. When we see a young person die — a teenager, a young adult, a middle-aged adult— we often talk about how untimely their death was, which implies to us that there must be a specific time in life when death is very appropriate and that would seem to be in old age.

This attitude toward the death of the young adult in the 18-30 year age bracket is a very interesting one. These are the years filled with a great deal of risk-taking: fast cars, experimentation with drugs and alcohol, and the like. Perhaps some of this behavior comes from the cultural attitudes we have toward death, toward war, toward violence. Part of it may come from that sense of invulnerability that young people often experience. We find that only as people get into their 30's, and perhaps their late 30's, do they begin to develop some well defined sense of the nature of death. Beginning at around 40, we find a new enlightenment exists. People begin to have an appreciation for the finiteness of life. The realization strikes us that, when we are 40, in all likelihood half of our life is over. Most of us in our 40's will now, if not earlier, face the death of a parent, and suddenly we begin to recognize the order of death: the oldest die first. Somewhere, at this time of life, perhaps, we become the oldest members of our own families, and hence we become the next in line to face death.

We also begin in our middle years to experience losses which can be termed partial deaths; our hearing is not as good as it was, we now need stronger glasses, we find ourselves moving more slowly, and we must maintain special diets. All of these represent to us partial losses, and each of these partial losses brings us a new realization about the sense of death as something that we ourselves are coming close to experiencing.

Finally, as we move into old age, whether we define that as 60 or 70 or some other chronological point in time, we find that philosophies about death become very significant and very important for us to look at and understand. Many theorists in the field of aging have proposed ideas that relate well to death and the elderly.

The Disengagement Theory, made popular by Elaine Cumming and William Henry (1961), suggested that in old age there is the sense and the desire to disengage ourselves from life, to become less involved, less active, and to remove ourselves slowly from all the activities around us. In effect, death becomes the ultimate disengagement. We begin, slowly, to leave our work, to disengage from friends, to disengage from our social activities and community responsibilities, as if we recognize that death is soon to be. The Disengagement Theory becomes one way of looking at death and the attitude of the elderly toward death.

The life review process, suggested by Robert Butler (1963), also has a relationship to death. Life review is triggered in individuals by the recognition that they are reaching the end of their lives; death is near. Hence, elderly people begin to reminisce. They begin to relive past experiences, trying to look at them and re-evaluate them, seeing them in new perspectives, summarizing them and reaching new understandings of what their lives have been. If, in the life review process, the person is able to decide that he can live with himself — that is, he feels content with what his life has been — then he also finds it easier to die with himself. However, if that review of the past is an agonizing experience, one of distress and regrets, then the prospect of death becomes frightening and difficult for the person to endure.

In a similar way, Erik Erikson (1959) talks of the last stage of life as that of integrity versus despair. It is in this stage that somehow we begin to see the finality of life as helping to make life more precious. Our task in old age becomes that of achieving integrity. By integrity we are suggesting that people need to come to a sense of conviction that their lives had meaning and purpose, that the fact that they lived made a difference. They begin to see their lives as continuums between the past and future generations and as parts of the overall picture of history. For the individuals who cannot see the purpose and meaning in their lives, for individuals who have only a sense of uncompleted tasks and unsatisfied goals, there exists an extremely deep fear of death and a powerful sense of wanting to go back and start all over again.

How do we deal with elderly people and the issues related to death? Most of us show a strong reluctance to talk about death with elderly people. Why? In some cases it is embarrassment. By talking with older relatives about death, we have that fear that they might think that all we are looking at is our inheritance. For some of us, talking about death with an older person, or with anyone, is a reminder of our own death, and that makes us very uncomfortable. In many instances, we are simply afraid to talk to elderly people about death because we don't want to upset them, and we are afraid that bringing up such a topic will only upset them. Finally, perhaps, we don't talk with the elderly about death because we don't want to lose them, and it becomes very difficult for us to deal with the fact that these people will die one day and leave us. We still find, interestingly enough, that in many books in the field of aging, very little time is devoted to the issues related to death. Perhaps that represents our lack of knowledge in the area, or perhaps it represents this general reluctance we have to associate death with old age. In reality, the elderly are willing to talk. If given a chance, they can and will unburden themselves of their thoughts about death. They will not talk continually, but they will keep bringing it up until someone listens. They have concerns. They want to know what to do with their possessions and their wealth. They want to arrange their funerals. They want to say their good-byes. It is important for us to give them the opportunities to say and do these things. The elderly do not become obsessed with death. Only when they do not have someone who is willing to talk with them do we find them continually mentioning the subject. As soon as someone responds to their concerns, the apparent need to talk about death will disappear.

Another important issue in working with elderly people is the issue of grief. One of the major difficulties of old age for many people is the fact of loneliness. Elderly people are often more isolated within their homes and communities, living at distances from relatives, and that produces a sense of loneliness. Death intensifies that loneliness. Most older people have had many losses of significant others: spouse, parents, many friends. It may even be that many of their own children have died. They experience tremendous amounts of grief. Many elderly people experience what Robert Kastenbaum (1977) suggests: bereavement overload. Before they can deal effectively with one grief experience, there is another one. Grief takes time to work through, and if deaths or other losses occur at such a rapid pace that we do not have time to deal with one loss before we must start dealing with the next loss, then we may well experience bereavement overload. This may happen to a younger person too, but in the earlier years of life, we have opportunities to find distractions for ourselves. Forty-year old individuals who experience many deaths still have work, travel, and other things that occupy some of their time, that in a sense take their minds away from their loss. For the elderly person, the isolated person, this is not the case. In such instances, the elderly griever may need special attention.

In general, as we come into contact with older people, we will find them exhibiting three basic attitudes toward death. For some, their attitude is one of becoming very upset with any talk of death. They prefer to have no one mention to them any issues related to death. They do not like to go to funerals of friends; they do not like to have anything to do with death. For others, we may find an attitude of just not allowing themselves to face the fact of death, and although it does not upset them, they simply put it off in the future, and at age 100, we still may find them making their plans without any real acceptance or recognition of the fact that death is soon to come. They don't become upset with discussions of death because they don't see it as applicable to them. Finally, we find those elderly people who have faced the prospect of death through a period of thinking and adjustment, who recognize that death is inevitable for them, that death is coming closer; they feel comfortable with that aspect of life experience. In the work we do with the elderly, we can help more individuals to develop this last attitude, to be able to see death as part of the inevitability of life and to help them in old age to feel comfortable with that prospect. This we can do by our willingness to talk, by our willingness to be open with them, by our willingness to deal with their feelings. As our society becomes more aware of the special needs and problems of the elderly, hopefully we will be better equipped to help them deal with issues related to death and dying.

REFERENCES AND/OR ADDITIONAL READINGS

Butler, R.N. (1963). The life review: An interpretation of reminiscences in the aged. *Psychiatry, 26,* 1, 65-76.

Cumming, E. & Henry, W.E. (1961). *Growing old.* New York: Basic Books.

Erikson, E.H. (1959). Identity and the life cycle: Selected papers. *Psychological Issues,* 1, 1-171.

Kastenbaum, R. (1977). Death and development through the lifespan. In H. Fiefel (Ed.). *New meanings of death.* New York: McGraw-Hill.

Wass, H. (1979). Death and the elderly. In H. Wass (Ed.). *Dying: Facing the facts.* Washington, D.C.: Hemisphere.

The Grief Process

When people do not do their "grief work" following a death, we may well find a serious mental, social, and emotional problem. The expression "grief work" is a very appropriate one. Overcoming a death, learning to go on without the love object, requires work. It is not something that just happens. In order to understand what the grief process is like, our starting point needs to be with some basic definitions.

Three words are often used interchangeably when discussing grief. Those words are *bereavement, grief,* and *mourning. Bereavement* refers to the event of loss in our lives. The fact that we are bereaved individuals identifies us as having a particular status, one which represents a deprivation caused by death or loss.

Grief represents an emotional response to a death or a loss and may include a variety of emotions. *Mourning* represents the process by which we deal with and resolve or handle our grief, the process by which we attempt to regain a balance in our internal world. Our concern with all three of these terms will center around grief.

Grief, as we can discuss it in terms of death, is actually a part of a much larger context of loss. We grieve over any loss we may experience, whether it be the death of a loved one, the day when our children leave home, or the loss experienced by retirement from our job. We grieve over loss through divorce, and we grieve over the loss of special material things.

What is the grief process like? Grief affects every aspect of our lives. It affects our physical make-up as well as our emotional and mental states; it affects our ability to relate to other people. First, grief can be seen as a physiological reaction. In 1944, Eric Lindemann suggested that there are varieties of physiological responses to death, things that many of us experience in a most common way. Examples of these physiological reactions include the loss of muscle power, our inability to do things physical, a subjective, empty feeling in the stomach, and tightness in the throat. All of these are very real physical symptoms experienced by the grieving individual. Physiologically, the griever is at high risk, and we find that, in most categories of grievers, mortality rates rise among individuals who have recently experienced a death as opposed to a group of similar individuals who are not coping with this loss. Studies (Rees and Luthins, 1967) have found mortality rates during the first year of bereavement to be seven times higher than in the general population. Other researchers have found significantly higher rates of chronic diseases among the recently bereaved (Carr and Schoenberg, 1970).

Psychologically, grief is a process of searching. It

is an attempt to find the missing person, an attempt to restore our world to what it was before our loss. It is a process of learning to withdraw the emotional investment and involvement we had in someone and presumably to place that emotion into someone or something else. One of the extreme difficulties for many grieving individuals is the fact that we discourage the opportunity for them to express their emotions directly. Hence, internally, there is a great deal of emotional upheaval; however, externally, there is an attempt to maintain control. This may often lead to problems since grief that is improperly expressed, managed, or dealt with can, in the long run, totally change the personality.

Finally, grief has a social nature. When we experience a death, it means the end of a particular human relationship. Part of the grief process, then, is finding a way in which we can break those ties to the other person. It is almost a rite of passage just as so many aspects of adolescence represents a rite of passage. Grief is also social in the sense that one of the things that can most assist us in the grief process is having the support of other people and of social groups, people with whom we can identify and to whom we can go for help.

Although grief is a universal experience, no two people experience grief the same way. The way in which our grief will be expressed, the way in which our grief will be felt, is affected by a variety of issues. First, our grief may be affected by the amount of pre-grieving we have done prior to the death. Pre-grieving can be seen in a variety of different relationships. Most of us, for example, have, in one way or another, pre-grieved the death of our grandparents or parents. It is the natural order of things for older persons to die first. Hence, when grandparents and parents die, we grieve, but our grief may not be as great as if the natural order failed: that is, if one of our children died first. We do not pre-grieve that kind of loss. Perhaps one of the reasons that women deal better with grief than do men, on the whole, is that women go through a process we might term "rehearsal in black," recognizing that, according to the statistics, they will probably live longer than their husbands. Hence, the death of a husband, although a tragedy, is somewhat expected. On the other hand, men do not expect to outlive their wives, and when a wife dies first, the grief experience may be much greater for the male.

Secondly, grief may be affected by the suddenness of the loss. This, to some degree, is related to what we call anticipatory grief. When a loved one goes through a terminal illness, and we have the opportunity to witness the slow decline in their health and being, we, in a sense, are already grieving. We begin, perhaps, to rehearse the death: we begin to decide what it will be like without them; we begin, in some ways, to prepare for the death.

So, when the individual dies, although we may grieve, we recover from our grief faster because of the expected nature of the loss. When, however, death occurs suddenly, as in an accident or heart attack, and there has been no opportunity to begin the grief process, we have no preparation or anticipation. Thus, grief may take much longer and be much more intense at that time.

The personality of the griever is a third factor affecting the grief process. Some of us, throughout our lives, have learned well how to cope with losses, and when we experience a death, which is one form of loss, we are able to cope with it very well. Other individuals find themselves devastated by almost any loss, and death, being the permanent, significant loss that it is, has a tremendous effect.

A fourth factor affecting grief is the strength of the attachment we have to the person who died. As we might expect, our grief will be very intense when the loss is of a person whom we loved very much and with whom we had an excellent relationship. However, we may similarly grieve over a death that ends a relationship that was not perfect. In those cases, we are grieving over what we hoped could have been, what we wished for, or the change in the relationship that we expected over time. This grief may be, for some individuals, more intense than in the good relationship where there are not a number of regrets and wishes.

Fifth, grief may be affected by what we term "object substitution." When we lose someone to death, how intensely and in what ways we grieve may be affected by whether or not there is something to substitute for our loss. It may well be that a younger woman with children will overcome her grief somewhat more rapidly than one who has no children and no other individuals in whom to invest the tremendous amount of love and concern that she has put previously into the dead person. A woman who may be pregnant at the time of the death of her husband may come through her grief, in part, because the birth of a new child represents a way to go on living and, in a sense, to see the dead individual in that child. However, some people search too strongly for an object to replace the lost person; a family, for example, may think the best thing to do upon the death of their child is to adopt a child immediately so that they can give that child the love they had for their own child. In those cases, object substitutions may actually impede the grief process, seemingly giving the individual a way out, but the grief is merely buried temporarily. Sooner or later, an intense sense of loss over the person who died still emerges. The deliberate search for a substitute love object should not begin until the grief work is well under way.

A sixth factor which can affect the grief process is the potential we saw in the individual who died. In most instances, we grieve more intensely over the death of a young person than we do over that of an old person. As we confront the death of a young person, we tend to reflect on all of our hopes for that person, the life that he or she could have had, the experiences he or she will never have. In the death of an older person, we tend to be less devastated, reminiscing back on the good life the individual had experienced and recognizing that the individual's life was full. Robert Fulton (1974) refers to that first case as a high grief experience in which there may be intense emotional reaction, as opposed to the latter which is a low grief experience in which we show less devastation, and in general, our grief seems to be less severe.

A seventh factor in grief is the way in which a death occurs. The grief response in the case where an individual dies from a long, terminal illness may, in part, be one of relief. When we must face a sudden death by heart attack, grief will be quite different from that felt as the result of a sudden death brought on by a homocide or a suicide, in which we can experience all kinds of anger, guilt and questions.

Our exposure to "little deaths" is an eighth factor affecting grief. Throughout our lives we are faced with continual losses. As we learn to cope with those losses, and as we have dealt with many of those losses, death may simply become an additional loss in the whole process of little deaths and our accumulation of experiences.

Finally, grief may be affected by our perception of the unfinished business that remains, unfinished business in the sense of failure to close relationships with the dead person. The unfinished business is more often an issue in sudden deaths than in the case of terminal illness where there has been an opportunity to close relationships and complete issues. Where such unfinished business exists, counseling may become necessary to help the bereaved deal with their grief.

What is the grief process like? For many years different authors have described the grief process as a variety of stages and concepts. One author may use three stages to describe grief, and another may use ten. All of these represent the grief process, but in slightly different ways of defining the reactions that go on during grief. Robert Kavanaugh (1972) suggests what may be a very appropriate model for us to examine, one which involves seven stages of grief. It seems to provide a useful delineation of the grief process, thus enabling us to understand more fully what may be happening to an individual at any given point in time. As with all stage theories, we must recognize that stages do not always work for every person, and we cannot assume that everyone will follow the expected pattern. Nevertheless, the stages do give us some point of departure for our understanding of grief.

The first stage that Kavanaugh suggests is that

of shock. In the shock stage, the individual may well experience fainting, emotional explosions, or bizarre behavior. It is a period of time during which the real and the unreal tend to collide. It is a period of disbelief and denial, an inability to recognize that death truly did occur. All too often, in the helping role, we try to use words, advice, and explanations with an individual who is in this shock phase, but these really don't work. Words are not heard. Explanations don't seem to help, nor do drugs or medication. All too often we fail to recognize that the grief process must be experienced. By providing the survivor with tranquilizers and other forms of medication, all we are doing is prolonging the process. We medicate individuals while much of their support system is present, and then in the weeks and months that follow, as much of the support system begins to disappear, the individuals come off the medication and then must experience the shock and all the other difficult aspects of the grief process. Only then, the individual is alone. The best thing we can do for individuals in shock is simply to be with them. Spend time with them. Be a support to them.

The second stage often experienced in the grief process is that of disorganization. In the disorganization stage, individuals simply can't seem to bring reality together. They engage in behavior that is totally out of character for them. They cannot seem to remember names. They may well threaten suicide. It is not a good time for an individual to make a decision. Unfortunately, grievers are often forced to make certain kinds of decisions while they are experiencing this sense of disorganization. At the very least, those decisions that can be put off temporarily should most definitely be delayed until the griever is in more stable condition. Encouraging a griever who is experiencing disorganization to sell the family home and move into a smaller place or live with children is inappropriate at this point in time. Individuals, as they continue into their grief process, may well decide at a later date that their decisions were made in haste and they are now unhappy with those decisions. Individuals in disorganization need opportunity to talk and to cry, and the talk must be on their part with no interruptions on our part to bring them back into some trace of reality. Again, the greatest help we can give most people who are experiencing disorganization is to stay with them to provide physical comfort in the sense of a touch, a caress, and a hug. These mean far more than words we may try to say.

The third stage Kavanaugh suggests is that of volatile emotions. This is a stage with which many of us who may be helping a grieving individual have a great deal of difficulty. In the volatile emotions stage, it would not be unusual to find the person first yelling, screaming, and cursing, and showing feelings of hatred and resentment. This is very difficult for most of us to deal with. Grieving individuals need a whipping post; they need someone upon whom they can take out their emotions, someone who will not desert them because of this need. They need to be allowed to express their emotions fully. Probably one of the things that can be most helpful to people with volatile emotions is a person who will engage in permissive listening, who will not try to bring too much sanity back to the situation at the moment, who will allow them to thrust out their feelings of anger, hatred, and blame, putting the responsibility for the death on the health care professional, on themselves, on the clergy, or on God. Feelings are not right or wrong. Feelings simply are. People should be given the opportunity to say and feel those things that are necessary for them to work through their grief.

The fourth stage is that of guilt. This is that period of time when the individual is looking for explanations and, most often, will put the issue of why the death occurred back on themselves. They are saying, in part, that if only they had gotten the deceased to a doctor sooner, if only they had not argued, if only they had not done thus and so. It appears as if the griever needs to do a time of penance, and all of our explanations and all of our pitying and providing of forgiveness do not seem to take away the guilt. The words may be important, but we must not become frustrated when individuals choose to maintain their guilt for a period of time. This stage will usually pass with time, but it has to be experienced by most.

In the fifth stage, we find a sense of loss and loneliness, a particularly painful time for the griever. This is the time when the griever walks into the house and sees the empty chair and bursts into tears or seems to hear footsteps that are not there. These are the feelings which may be experienced on holidays or anniversaries of the death: an extreme emptiness, a sense that one's world will never be the same again. This, too, needs to be experienced totally. We often make the mistake of trying immediately to fill the griever's and bereaved's environment again, offering them the opportunity or forcing them into going out again or developing new relationships. Those actions may be important at some period of time, but before the individuals are really ready to move on in their grief, they need to have that sense of how alone they feel and how extreme their sense of loss is. Good, stabilizing friends can help a great deal by their physical presence, by giving the person the opportunity to talk, by not trying to change the subject in order to take the griever's mind off the dead person, by not forcing them to give away and put away objects and reminders. These are things that bereaved individuals must do in their own time and in their own way.

Next, frequently comes the stage of relief. Somehow, the extreme pain has stopped, and although the grief has not disappeared, at least we begin to feel better. One of the interesting things that can happen in the relief phase is that, as we begin to feel better, we return to a sense of guilt over feeling better. Somehow our world should not return to normal. We feel that we shouldn't be forgetting, and so we almost take ourselves out of relief and put ourselves back into some of those earlier stages, but in a less intense way.

Finally will come the stage of reestablishment. It does not happen overnight. It takes a period of time, but it represents that point in time when the griever is able to put away the mementoes of the past and to begin to return to the real world, to establish new relationships, to pick up old relationships, and to move on in life. There is no real timetable for this grief process. In most individuals we will see the intense experession of grief last for periods of weeks to months or even a year. Experience tells us that for most people the grief process will take a period of approximately two years, but indeed, it will vary from one person to another. Even when people have recovered from their grief and have reached the point of reestablishment, it is important to remember that grief never goes away. We will continue to grieve over the death of someone close to us for the rest of our lives, but the grief is no longer the great disrupter. It is something that appears periodically through certain events, through certain people; we are reminded of the dead person and some of the feeling of loss comes flowing back to us, but it subsides much more rapidly than it did before.

It was mentioned earlier that grief may be affected by the way in which a person dies. It would seem appropriate to make a few comments about some particularly difficult types of death situations and the resulting grief which accompanies these situations. Each year in the United States, approximately 10,000 children die from what we refer to as Sudden Infant Death Syndrome (SIDS); (Bergman, et al. 1974). A young child dies for no apparent reason. This type of death situation provokes some very intense grief and particular difficulties for the grief process. As we might expect, the death of a child is always difficult. In a SIDS death, since there is no apparent cause of the death, there is a tendency on the part of the parents to look for someone to hold responsible for that death. In some instances, it may be a babysitter if, indeed, the child died when the parents were not at home. In some instances, there may even be blame placed on other children, a feeling that they were not taking their responsibility in caring for the younger brother or sister. In most cases, however, the sense of responsibility and blame passes from one parent to the other, and we begin to see a great deal of difficulty in the relationship between the mother and father, often leading to separation and divorce. It is important in SIDS deaths that we give the parents an opportunity to deal with their grief, a time to hold the dead child, not rushing them out of the emergency room, encouraging them to talk, sitting with them, taking time to help in any tangible way in which we can. Often, in this kind of death, we need to provide opportunities for the parents to receive counseling, both over the loss they have experienced as well as marriage counseling of some kind to deal with the emotions they are experiencing within the marriage itself.

Death by suicide is another example of a special kind of death. Suicide represents a sudden death, but more specifically, suicide often represents a death in which we have a tremendous sense of guilt; somehow the survivor could have prevented this death from happening. We must deal with the survivors' sense of guilt that they place on themselves and, again, with a certain degree of blame that they may well place on someone else. Moreover, we need to recognize that, in suicide situations, there may also be a need and a reluctance on the part of the survivors to place responsibility on the individual who is dead. Hence, they may have feelings of anger toward the dead person and questions such as, "How could you do this to me?" but they feel as though it is inappropriate to express that kind of anger to one who has died. They need to understand that these feelings of anger are natural and justified and certainly must not be suppressed.

Deaths by homicide are another example of a special kind of death situation. Frequently, when there has been a homicide, the grief reaction is considerably delayed. Survivors often seem unable to express their grief because of the tremendous sense of rage and anger in which they are involved. It seems that the grief never really begins fully until the individual who has committed the murder has been caught and brought to trial. And since, in our justice system today, trials and appeals last for a long period of time, we often find individuals and families whose grief lasts much longer than under normal types of death situations.

How do people express their grief? What are some of the styles of grieving that we may find in individuals? There are probably as many styles of grieving as there are people who grieve. Generally, we can recognize a few basic things that people do and ways in which they show their grief. For some people, their grief is controlled primarily by their strong religious statements, and consequently, although they have experienced a sense of loss, their loss is tempered by their feeling of assurance that the dead individual is in a far better place and no longer suffers but rather is at peace. Sometimes we find almost no grief expressed in individuals because their relationship to the dead person had been minimal over recent years. They may have lived at a great distance, or they have had little contact with the person. Some individuals deal with their grief almost by creating a shrine to the dead person. You can walk into their homes and find rooms undisturbed and untouched since the day the person died. This may be a negative factor for some, but it need not be as long as this does not go too far. Grief may be expressed by some people through the use of rituals and ceremonies. This seems to be very helpful for many people, and even for those who may be continuing to grieve a long time after a death, perhaps designing or re-creating a ritual or ceremony like a rite of passage may help them to cope far better with their grief. Some survivors deal with their grief by assuming some of the characteristics of the person who died: attitudes, beliefs and values, for example. We might find a married couple, each person belonging to a different political party, but following a death, the survivor changes his or her political affiliation to the party of the deceased. Taking on the attitudes of the deceased as our own is one way of keeping the dead person alive. Sometimes we find people who manage their grief by becoming exceedingly active, in fact almost losing themselves in a variety of activities and things that keep their lives very filled. Some people do this in a positive way of finding very healthy activity outlets, while others may lose themselves in a life filled with trivia and meaningless kinds of activity. Some people deal with their grief in a kind of severe depression, and these are individuals who may often need professional assistance and will welcome the recommendation from someone else that perhaps some professional help may be in order. For these individuals we may be dealing with what may be termed pathological grief.

Pathological grief occurs whenever grief becomes so intense that it interferes with an individual's ability to function in the day-to-day world. Hence, people who for months following the death are unable to take care of their children, who are unable to return to work, or who sit alone constantly in tears and have really separated themselves almost entirely from the rest of the world may well be experiencing pathological grief and need some assistance. Furthermore, individuals who show no grief over a major loss in their lives, and yet in whom we can sense a number of difficulties and a failing to deal with their loss, may be experiencing pathological grief.

Why does grief become pathological? It may be due to the personality of the griever. It may be due to some unresolved element in the previous relationship with the dead person. There are all kinds of things that cause pathological grief. We find pathological grief, for example, in cases of multiple deaths, where several members of a family may have all died at one time, and it is as if there is such a tremendous amount of grief that we are just unable to deal with it. On the other hand, there may be pathological grief over a death that somehow is not seen by others as significant. We may have a very elderly grandparent who dies, one with whom we were very close, and yet society's response to us is, "They had a full life and it was time for them to die." We feel somehow as though permission has not been given to us to have our grief and to be honest in the grief that we are experiencing. Sometimes pathological grief may result because the death itself was such a socially unacceptable loss. Suicide often produces this response in survivors. Since society fails to understand why an individual may choose suicide and looks upon some of the survivors with a sense of blame and responsibility and questioning, grievers may not deal honestly and openly with their loss and may need some professional assistance.

Some people develop pathological grief because they have tried to remain too strong for too long a period of time. For example, we find that in many deaths in a family, the male takes on the figure of the strong one for a period of time and is very concerned with how others in the family will cope and survive and so internalizes his grief and fails to go through his own expressions of grief. Then, finally, as other members of the family begin to recover, the grief overwhelms that strong one, and now they grieve at a time when everyone else seems to have completed their grief. They may need a certain amount of professional help.

We must be careful not to over-react to grief and to assume that grief is pathological based on a cursory examination. That is to say, grief does differ from person to person, and what we see in one individual, although it may be a more intense and more difficult grief experience than that to be observed in another, does not necessarily make it pathological. We must reserve our judgment until we see how individuals are functioning and how they feel about the way in which they are functioning.

How can we best handle our own grief experiences? Each of us must find the right method for ourselves. There are some things that become a common part of learning to overcome the grief process. First and foremost, there is a need for us to accept our grief, not to try to be brave but rather to allow ourselves to experience the sense of loss that we indeed have. We need to learn to talk about it and we need to take care of ourselves in the grief process. We need to be concerned for our health. We must eat properly, we must exercise properly, and we must deal with our own physical needs as we go through the grief. We need to take some time to review the relationship we had with the dead person and to begin to put our relationship into perspective, to be able to weigh the good and the bad, and to be able to find some sense of closure in the relationship. We need to find some outlet for ourselves which may involve work, new groups of people, or some kind of activity, something that allows us to invest the emotional energy which was invested in the deceased. We need to take that energy and place it into some other person or activity or event. In a sense, we must try to turn our grief into a creative sort of energy.

Some people can be greatly helped by recording their thoughts or by keeping a diary or a journal. This is a way to get their feelings out, feelings they may not be able to express to someone else. Grieving people need to postpone making major decisions. The time will be appropriate to make these decisions later, but now is probably not the time, and we need to learn to postpone those great decisions. We need to verbalize our guilt feelings. In almost any relationship, when the relationship ends, be it by divorce, death or otherwise, there is some degree of guilt. Perhaps, in order to overcome the grief in death, we need to express what our guilt feelings are. That seems to be the only way in which we can work on that grief process. We also need to learn not to be afraid to seek help from others. Grief is one of the most intense emotional experiences any of us will ever have. All of us will experience grief. Most of us really cannot do it alone. We must not be afraid to seek help from others, whether it be relatives, close friends, or, if the need arises, from professionals. Finally, we can best deal with our grief if we learn to live one day at a time. Our grief will not go away overnight, but each day does get better.

What can we do to help someone else who is grieving? What can our role be? We can help another person who is grieving greatly by saying what we really feel, by not holding back, by trying to be understanding, by being with the person, and by developing our sensitivities to the situation and the emotions that the person must be feeling. We can help by being careful that we are not doing something to block the grief process. It is natural for us to want to get people back on their feet, to bring them into the real world, but to do so too quickly, to force the person back, does not help. We need to allow others the time they need to grieve. We do, at some point, need to encourage them to develop some new relationships, but that cannot be done too quickly. It takes time. We need to listen; we need to be there. We need to be willing to recommend to others groups that may be helpful for them. We have found that, even among professionals, we can only go so far in helping someone who is grieving, particularly since many of us have not experienced the same loss as this grieving individual may have. Yet there are groups of people who have gone through it, who can be helpful: programs such as Widow to Widow, Compassionate Friends, Candlelighters, Seasons, Gold Star Wives of America. There are many such groups which represent individuals who have experienced deaths in a particular way, and those groups can be a most helpful source for others who are now grieving.

Lastly, we need to recognize that to help someone grieve we need to risk ourselves. Whether we are professional caregivers or friends, we must risk personal involvement. We will all make mistakes. In the long run, however, it is better to try than never to have attempted to help. Grief is a devastating process which can take an individual from the peaks of life to the depths. Given time, if people are allowed to work through their grief, they will return to life as much stronger human beings than they ever were before.

REFERENCES AND/OR ADDITIONAL READINGS

Bergman, A., Melton, J., Baker, R. et al. (1974). *Sudden unexpected death in infants.* New York: MSS Information Corp.

Carr, A.C., & Schoenberg, B. (1970). Object-loss and somatic symptom formation. In B. Schoenberg et al. (Eds.). *Loss and Grief: Psychological management in medical practice.* New York: Columbia University Press.

Fulton, R. (1978). Death, grief and social recuperation. *Omega, 1,* 23-28.

Kavanaugh, R.E. (1972). *Facing death.* Los Angeles: Nash Publishing.

Kushner, H.S. (1981). *When bad things happen to good people.* New York: Schocken Books, Inc.

Lindemann, E. (1944). Symptomatology and management of acute grief. *American Journal of Psychiatry, 101,* 141-148.

Rees, W.D. & Luthins, S.G. (1967). The mortality of bereavement. *British Medical Journal, 4,* 13-16.

Afterword

Our attitudes toward death and dying are changing. We are becoming more aware of the special needs of dying people and grieving individuals and we are learning new ways to respond to these needs.

As our society becomes more "death conscious," there is always the danger that this new awareness and openness will become its own form of death denial.

It becomes the task of all of us, whether professional caregiver, loved one, or friend to see that we continue to deal with the concerns of the dying patient. We must allow them to remain in control of their lives and recognize that, although they are dying, they are, in reality, no different from us.

For the grieving person, we must continue to provide special care and support for as long as necessary. We can help them to grow from their loss to become stronger human beings.

We must provide opportunities for our children to be exposed to death and to understand death in their own way. Only in this way can we insure that our society will not return to an attitude of denial and hiding death.

Finally, for ourselves, we must make sure that the eventual certainty of our own death gives us a reason to live each day to its fullest. Hopefully we will all learn to experience each sunrise, each flower, each happy moment as something special in our lives. May none of us reach our final destination having to say, "Oh, how I've wasted my life."